Where in the World Can I . . .

VISIT A
RAINFOREST?

Where in the World Can I . . .

VISIT A
RAINFOREST?

WORLD
BOOK

www.worldbook.com

World Book, Inc.
180 North LaSalle Street, Suite 900
Chicago, Illinois 60601
USA

For information about other World Book publications, visit our website at **www.worldbook.com** or call **1-800-WORLDBK (967-5325).**

For information about sales to schools and libraries, call 1-800-975-3250 (United States), or 1-800-837-5365 (Canada).

Library of Congress Cataloging-in-Publication Data for this volume has been applied for.

Where in the World Can I…
ISBN: 978-0-7166-5251-9 (set, hc.)

Visit a Rainforest?
ISBN: 978-0-7166-5257-1 (hc.)
ISBN: 978-0-7166-5269-4 (pf.)

Also available as:
ISBN: 978-0-7166-5263-2 (e-book)

STAFF

Executive Committee
President
  Geoff Broderick

Vice President, Editorial
  Tom Evans

Vice President, Finance
  Donald D. Keller

Vice President, International
  Eddy Kisman

Vice President, Technology
  Jason Dole

Director, Human Resources
  Bev Ecker

Editorial
Senior Editor
  Shawn Brennan

Curriculum Designer
  Caroline Davidson

Proofreader
  Nathalie Strassheim

Graphics and Design
Senior Visual Communications Designer
  Melanie Bender

Coordinator, Design Development and Production
  Brenda Tropinski

Senior Media Editor
  Rosalia Bledsoe

Acknowledgments
Writer: Cynthia O'Brien

Produced by
Focus Strategic Communications Inc.

TABLE OF CONTENTS

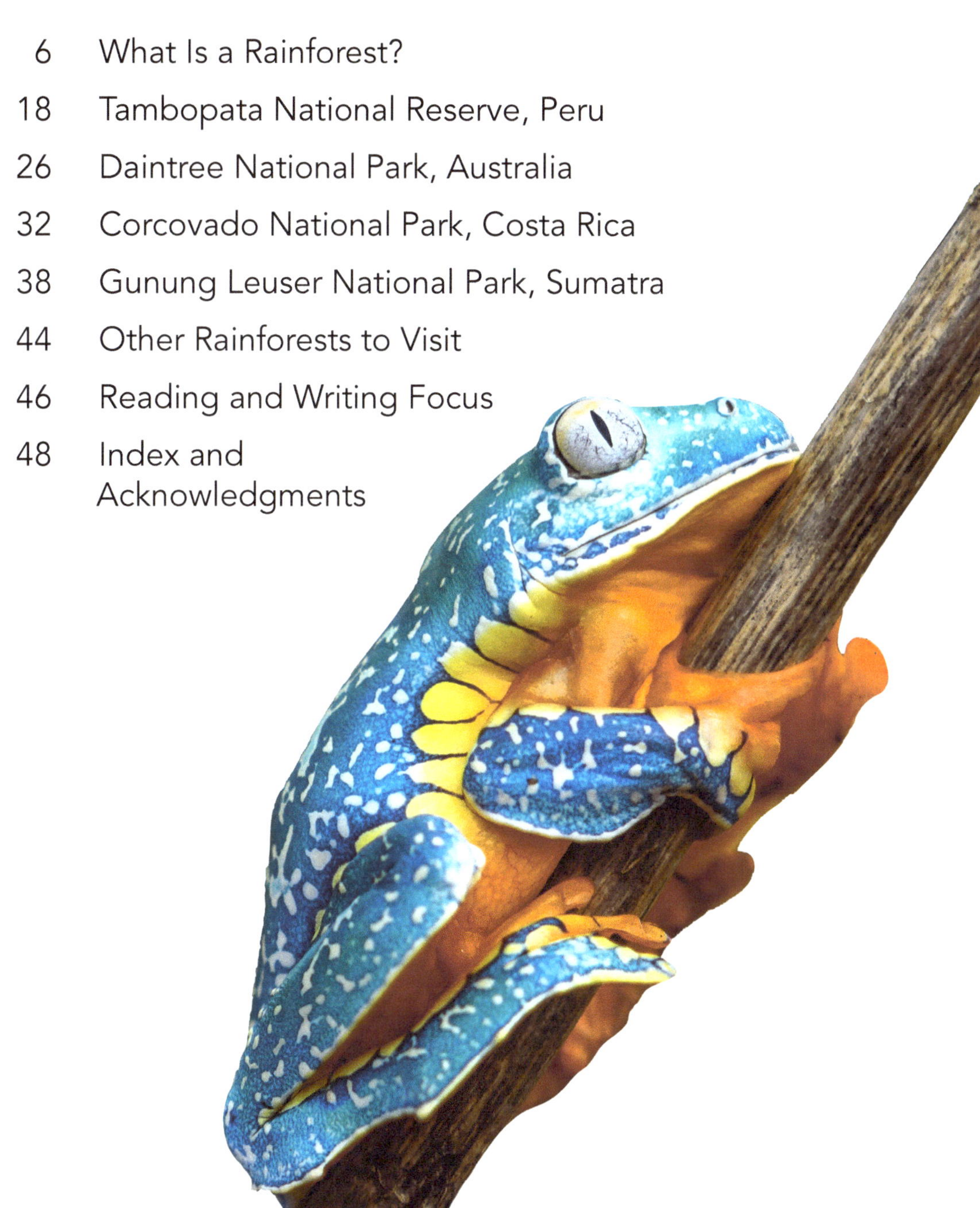

WHAT IS A
RAINFOREST?

A rainforest is an area of tall trees and plenty of rain. As much as 30 feet (9 meters) of rain may fall in one year. There are rainforests on every continent in the world except Antarctica. Rainforests are Earth's oldest *ecosystems* (areas made up of specific living and nonliving things). They have an amazing variety of plant and animal life. Half of the world's species live in rainforests, even though they cover just six percent of Earth's surface.

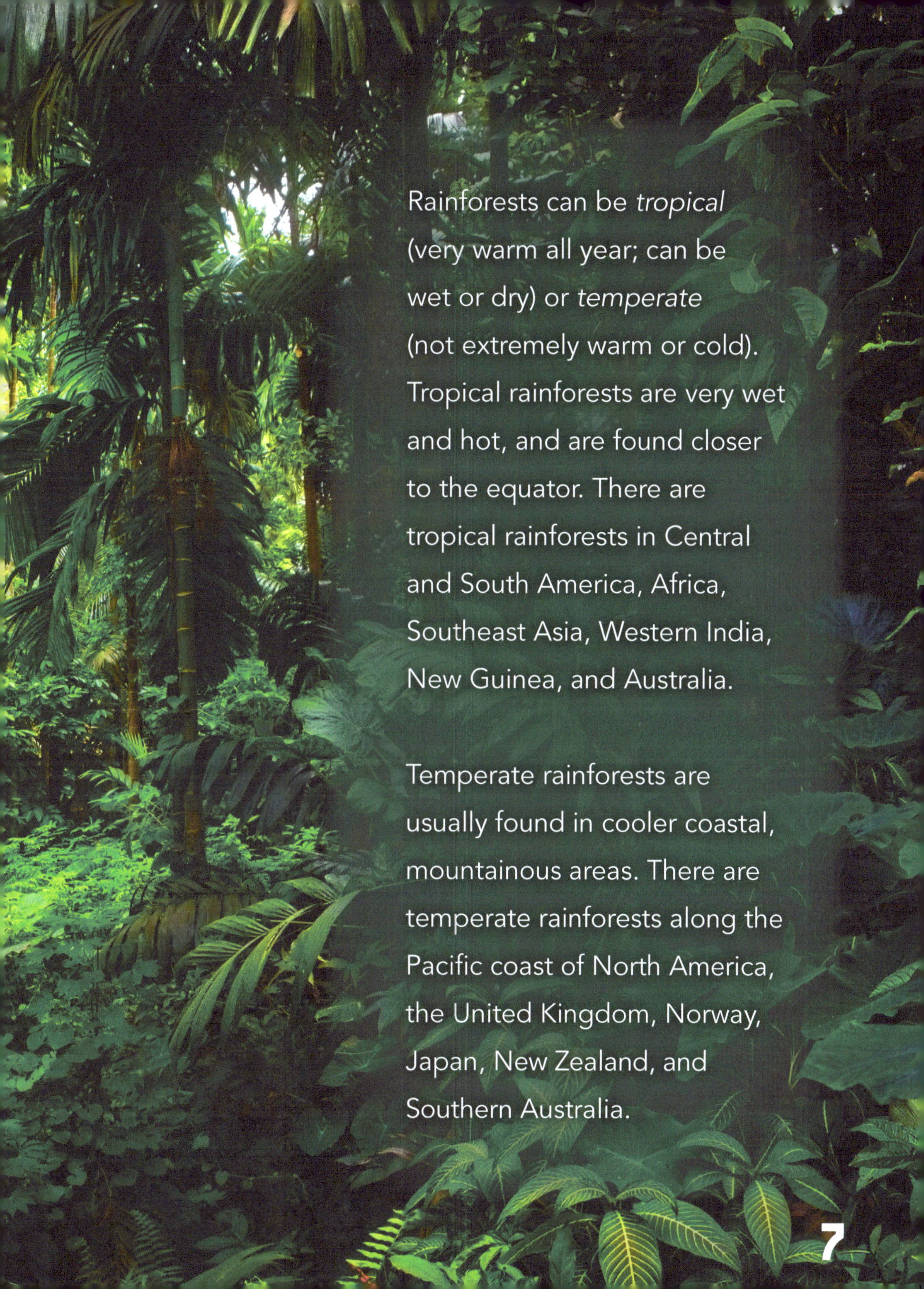

Rainforests can be *tropical* (very warm all year; can be wet or dry) or *temperate* (not extremely warm or cold). Tropical rainforests are very wet and hot, and are found closer to the equator. There are tropical rainforests in Central and South America, Africa, Southeast Asia, Western India, New Guinea, and Australia.

Temperate rainforests are usually found in cooler coastal, mountainous areas. There are temperate rainforests along the Pacific coast of North America, the United Kingdom, Norway, Japan, New Zealand, and Southern Australia.

Most rainforests have four layers: emergent, canopy, understory, and forest floor. The emergent layer is made up of the tallest trees in the forest. The tallest known tree grows in the Amazon and is almost 290 feet (88 meters) high! Birds, bats, and insects live in this layer.

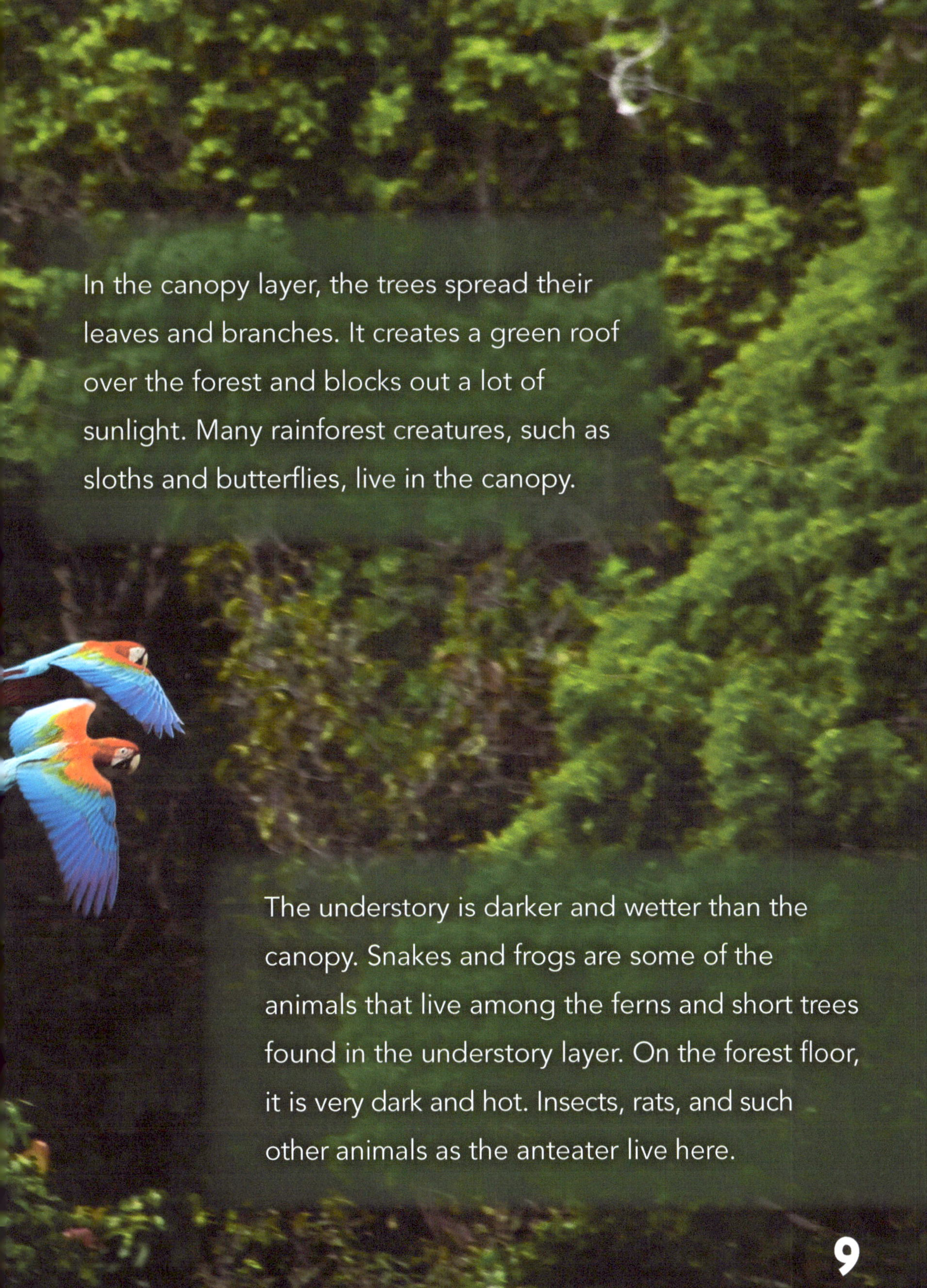

In the canopy layer, the trees spread their leaves and branches. It creates a green roof over the forest and blocks out a lot of sunlight. Many rainforest creatures, such as sloths and butterflies, live in the canopy.

The understory is darker and wetter than the canopy. Snakes and frogs are some of the animals that live among the ferns and short trees found in the understory layer. On the forest floor, it is very dark and hot. Insects, rats, and such other animals as the anteater live here.

The Amazon in South America is the world's largest
rainforest. The vast forest lies around the Amazon River,
the second longest river in the world after the Nile in Africa.
The Amazon rainforest covers an area of over 2.6 million
square miles (6 million square kilometers) and stretches
from eastern Brazil to the Andes Mountains in Peru.

Millions of species of animals live in the Amazon. Wildcats,
colorful birds, and many types of monkeys all live here.
There are snakes, lizards, and frogs that you will not find
anywhere else. You will also find rare butterflies and other
insects. About 40,000 plant species grow in the Amazon,
too. New species of animals
and plants are discovered
all the time in this
rainforest.

The world's second largest rainforest is the Congo in Africa. It surrounds the Congo River and spreads across six African countries, but most of the rainforest falls within the Democratic Republic of the Congo. Altogether, the Congo rainforest covers over 780 thousand square miles (2 million square kilometers) and contains about 10,000 types of tropical plants.

Some of the most *endangered* (at risk of dying out) animals in the world live in this rainforest, including forest elephants, gorillas, bonobos, and okapis.

Temperate rainforests are cooler than tropical forests. They receive less rain and less sunshine. Many of the trees in temperate rainforests are large old *coniferous* trees. These are trees, such as spruce, that have cones and needle-like leaves.

Some trees are *deciduous*, which means they lose their leaves in the fall. The lush plant life in these forests typically includes mosses and ferns.

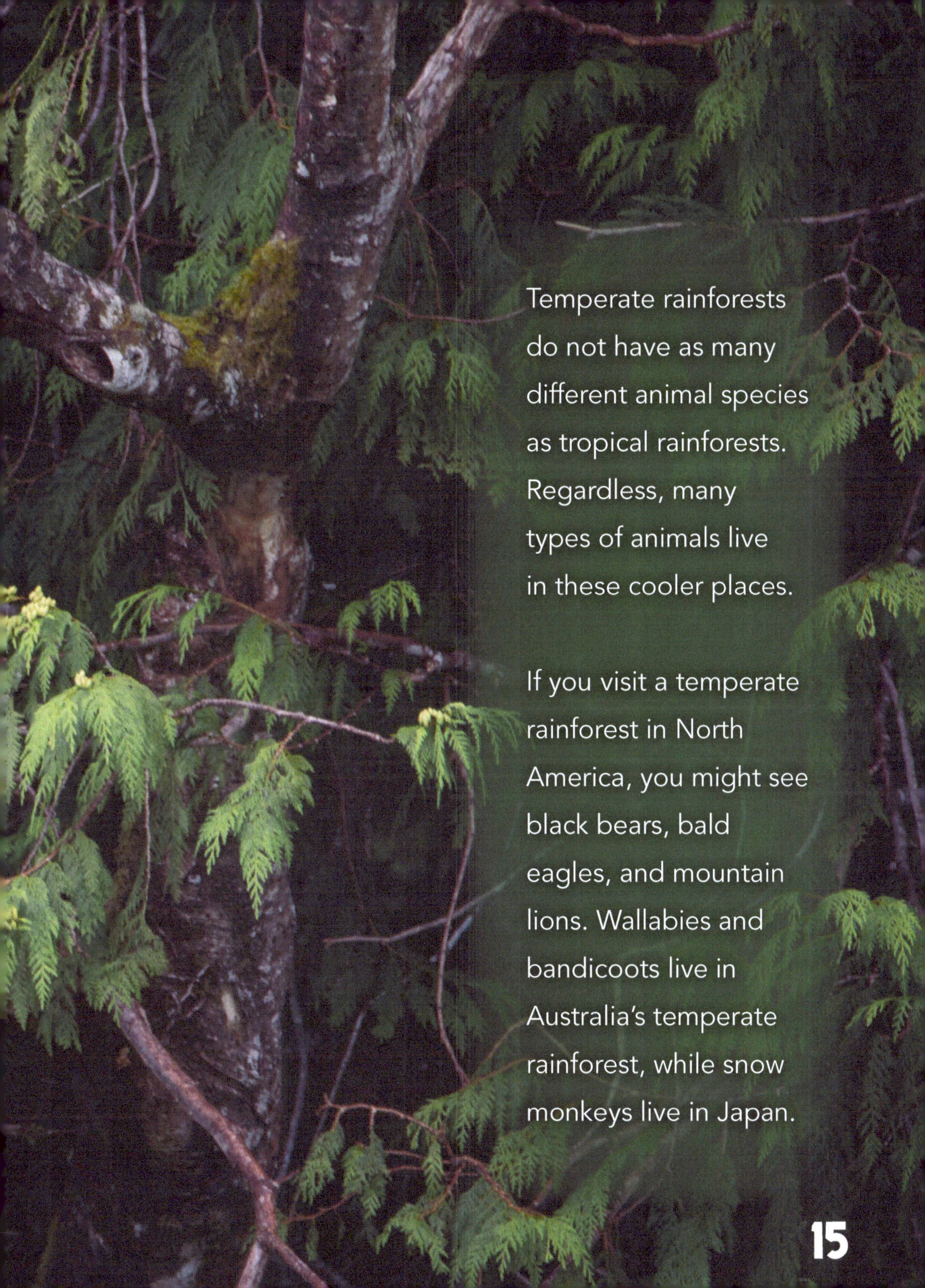

Temperate rainforests
do not have as many
different animal species
as tropical rainforests.
Regardless, many
types of animals live
in these cooler places.

If you visit a temperate
rainforest in North
America, you might see
black bears, bald
eagles, and mountain
lions. Wallabies and
bandicoots live in
Australia's temperate
rainforest, while snow
monkeys live in Japan.

The world's rainforests are crucial to the future of the planet. Rainforests produce oxygen and absorb carbon. Storing carbon helps to reduce *greenhouse gases*. These are gases in Earth's atmosphere that trap heat and cause the planet to warm up.

Rainforests also help to keep Earth's water cycles healthy, and they take in the sun's energy to help keep Earth's temperatures stable. They supply many kinds of fruit, wood, and plants for medicines. Rainforests are home to millions of the world's animals and plants.

Sadly, humans have destroyed massive areas of rainforest. People are clearing the land for farming, such industries as mining, and raising *livestock* (animals reared for food).

Visiting rainforests is helpful because it encourages countries to protect them. Keep reading to discover where in the world you can explore some incredible rainforests.

TAMBOPATA NATIONAL RESERVE, PERU

The Tambopata
National Reserve in
southeastern Peru,
east of Cusco,
includes part of the
lowland Amazon rainforest.
It covers 1,061 square miles
(2,748 square kilometers) and protects a
remarkable array of animals and plants.

There are over 100 species of mammals, over
1,200 types of plants, and at least
1,200 kinds of butterflies. There are
also huge numbers of other insects,
as well as birds, reptiles, and *amphibians*
(*am FIHB ee uhns*)—animals, such as frogs,
that live in both water and on land.

You can explore some of the reserve by taking a boat on Lake Sandoval or the Tambopata River. As you float along the water, you will see birds in the trees on shore. Look out for giant otters or river turtles swimming nearby.

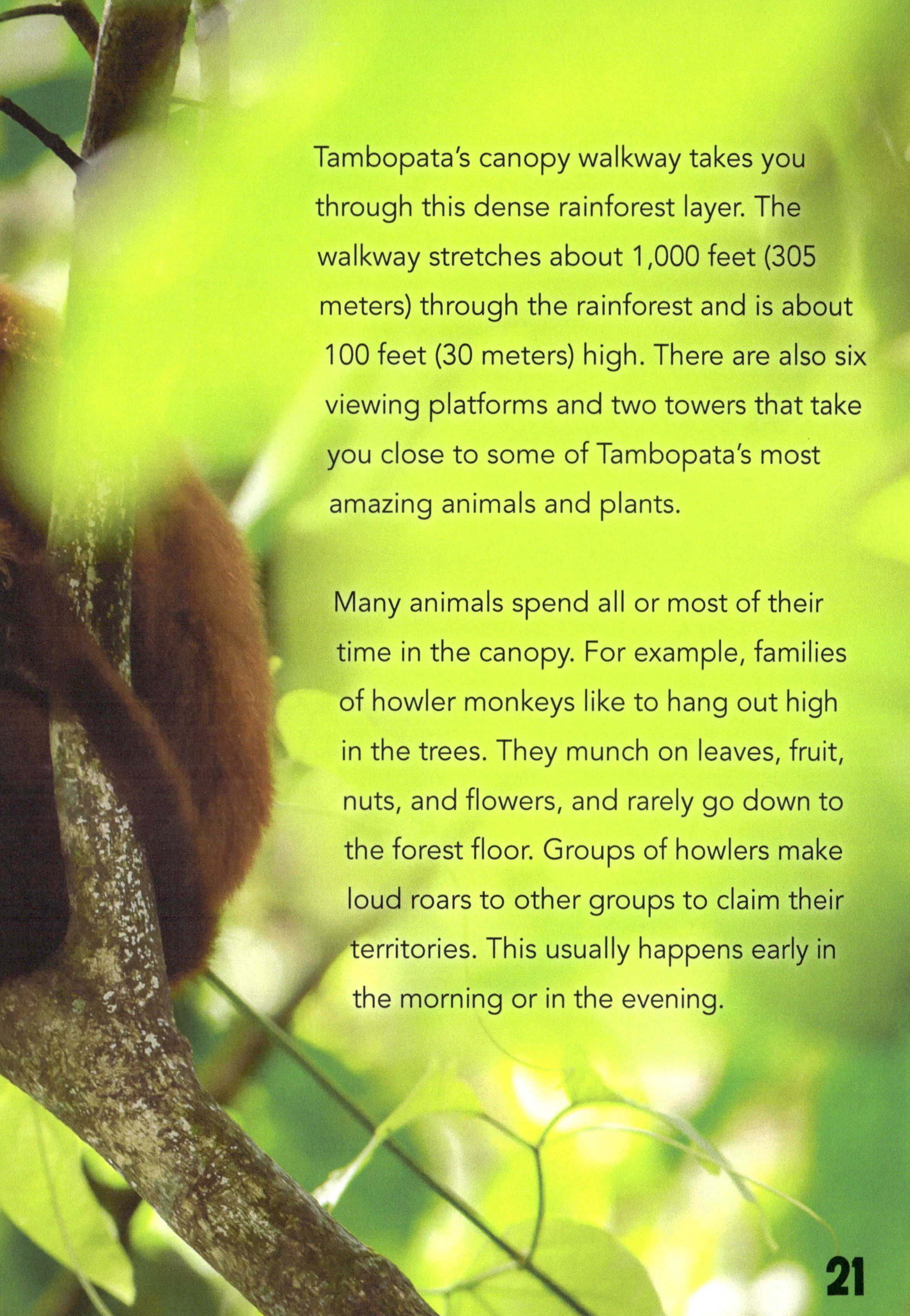

Tambopata's canopy walkway takes you through this dense rainforest layer. The walkway stretches about 1,000 feet (305 meters) through the rainforest and is about 100 feet (30 meters) high. There are also six viewing platforms and two towers that take you close to some of Tambopata's most amazing animals and plants.

Many animals spend all or most of their time in the canopy. For example, families of howler monkeys like to hang out high in the trees. They munch on leaves, fruit, nuts, and flowers, and rarely go down to the forest floor. Groups of howlers make loud roars to other groups to claim their territories. This usually happens early in the morning or in the evening.

One of the most exciting animals to see on your visit to Tambopata is the jaguar. These large wildcats look similar to leopards, but there are several differences. For example, both species have markings called rosettes (so named because the black spots form a circle, like a rose). But a jaguar's rosettes have spots inside them, whereas a leopard's do not.
The Amazon rainforest is also home to the ocelot, but visitors rarely see these shy cats. Ocelots are active at night and like to stay inside the dense forest.

You may see a jaguar lurking by the riverbank looking for food. They are fierce hunters and will attack most animals, including caimans and tapirs. Caimans are related to alligators and prey on all kinds of animals, including jaguars! The black caiman is the biggest creature in the caiman family. Tapirs are very large animals with a tube-like nose similar to a small elephant trunk. In fact, tapirs are related to horses and rhinoceroses.

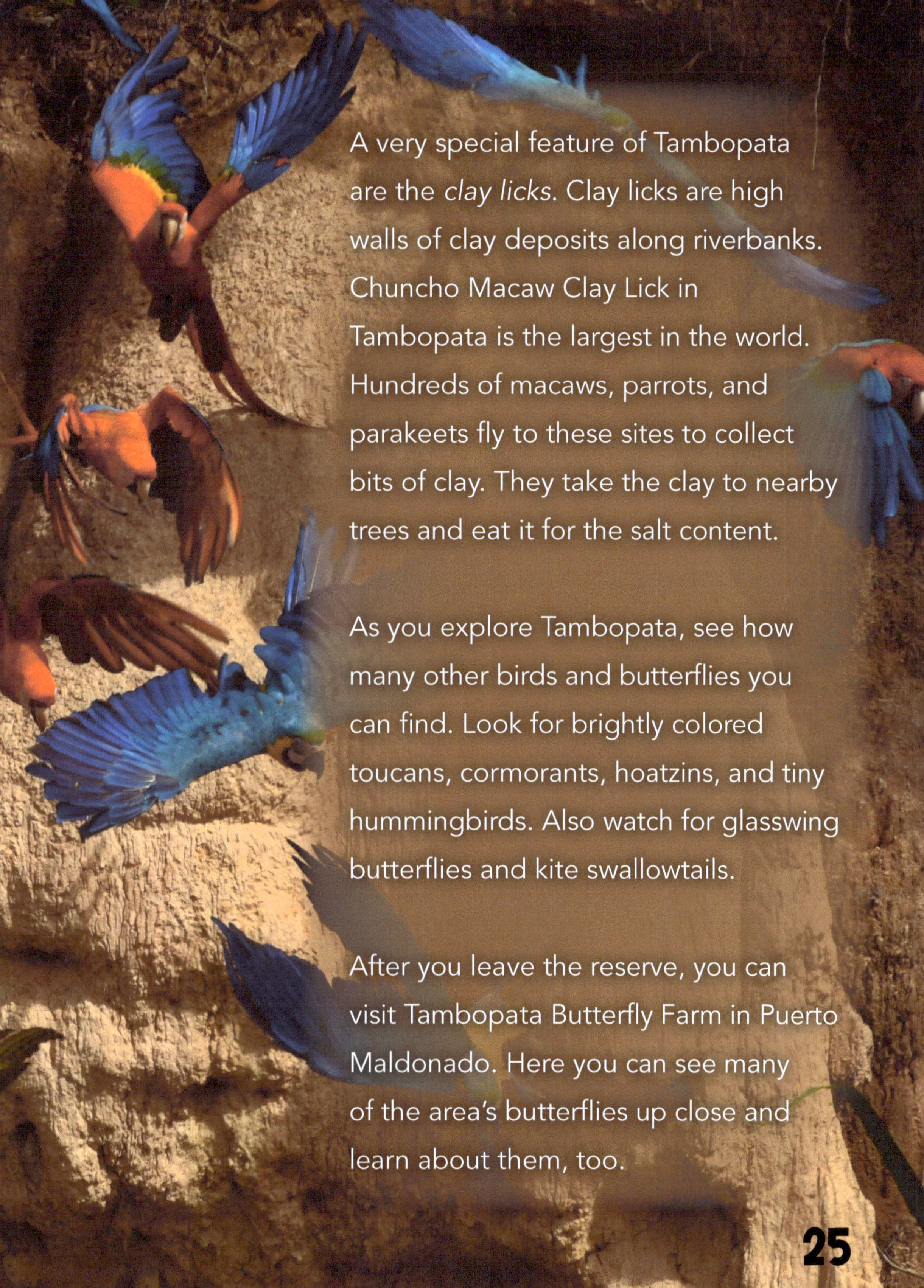

A very special feature of Tambopata are the *clay licks*. Clay licks are high walls of clay deposits along riverbanks. Chuncho Macaw Clay Lick in Tambopata is the largest in the world. Hundreds of macaws, parrots, and parakeets fly to these sites to collect bits of clay. They take the clay to nearby trees and eat it for the salt content.

As you explore Tambopata, see how many other birds and butterflies you can find. Look for brightly colored toucans, cormorants, hoatzins, and tiny hummingbirds. Also watch for glasswing butterflies and kite swallowtails.

After you leave the reserve, you can visit Tambopata Butterfly Farm in Puerto Maldonado. Here you can see many of the area's butterflies up close and learn about them, too.

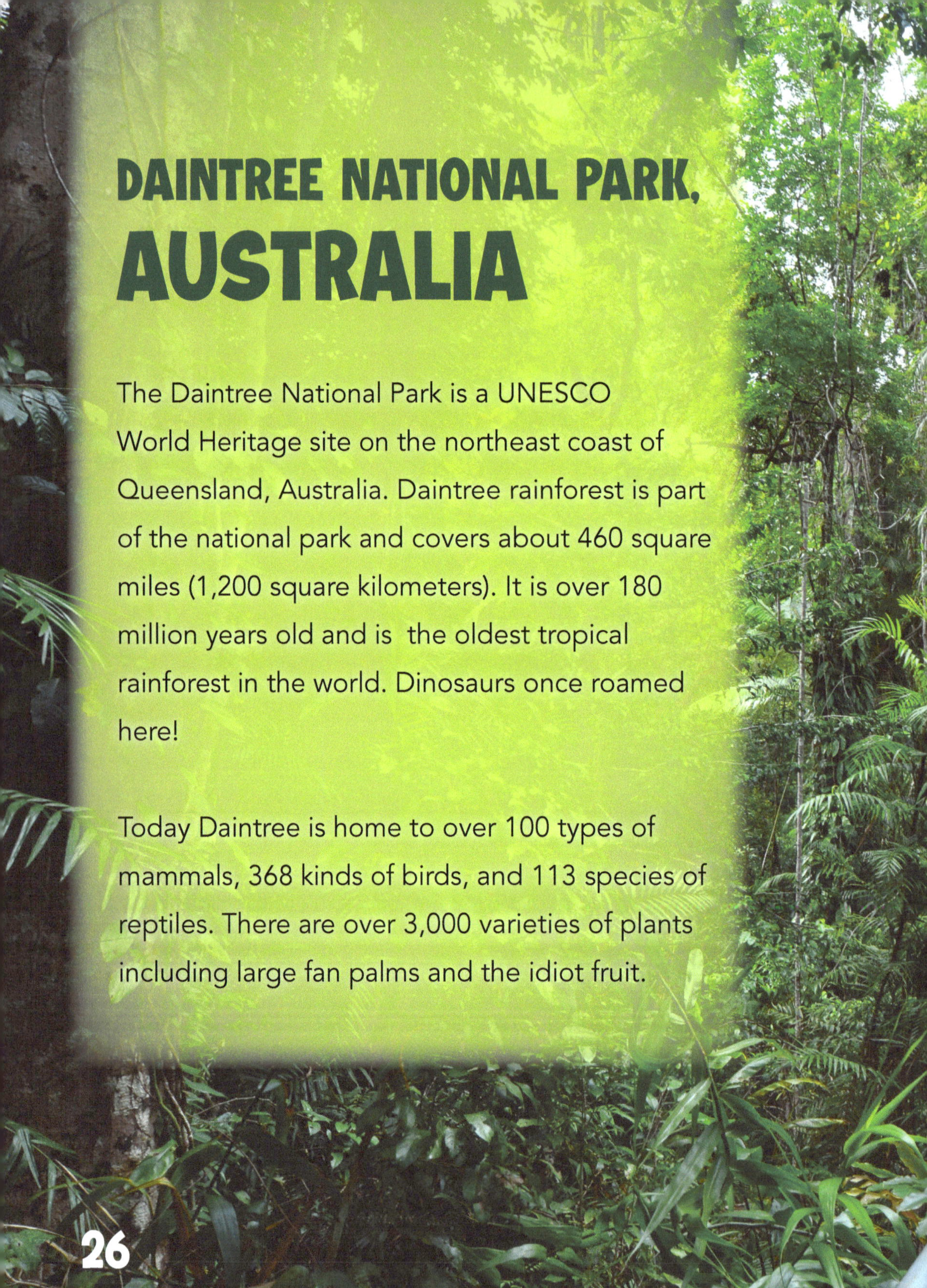

DAINTREE NATIONAL PARK,
AUSTRALIA

The Daintree National Park is a UNESCO World Heritage site on the northeast coast of Queensland, Australia. Daintree rainforest is part of the national park and covers about 460 square miles (1,200 square kilometers). It is over 180 million years old and is the oldest tropical rainforest in the world. Dinosaurs once roamed here!

Today Daintree is home to over 100 types of mammals, 368 kinds of birds, and 113 species of reptiles. There are over 3,000 varieties of plants including large fan palms and the idiot fruit.

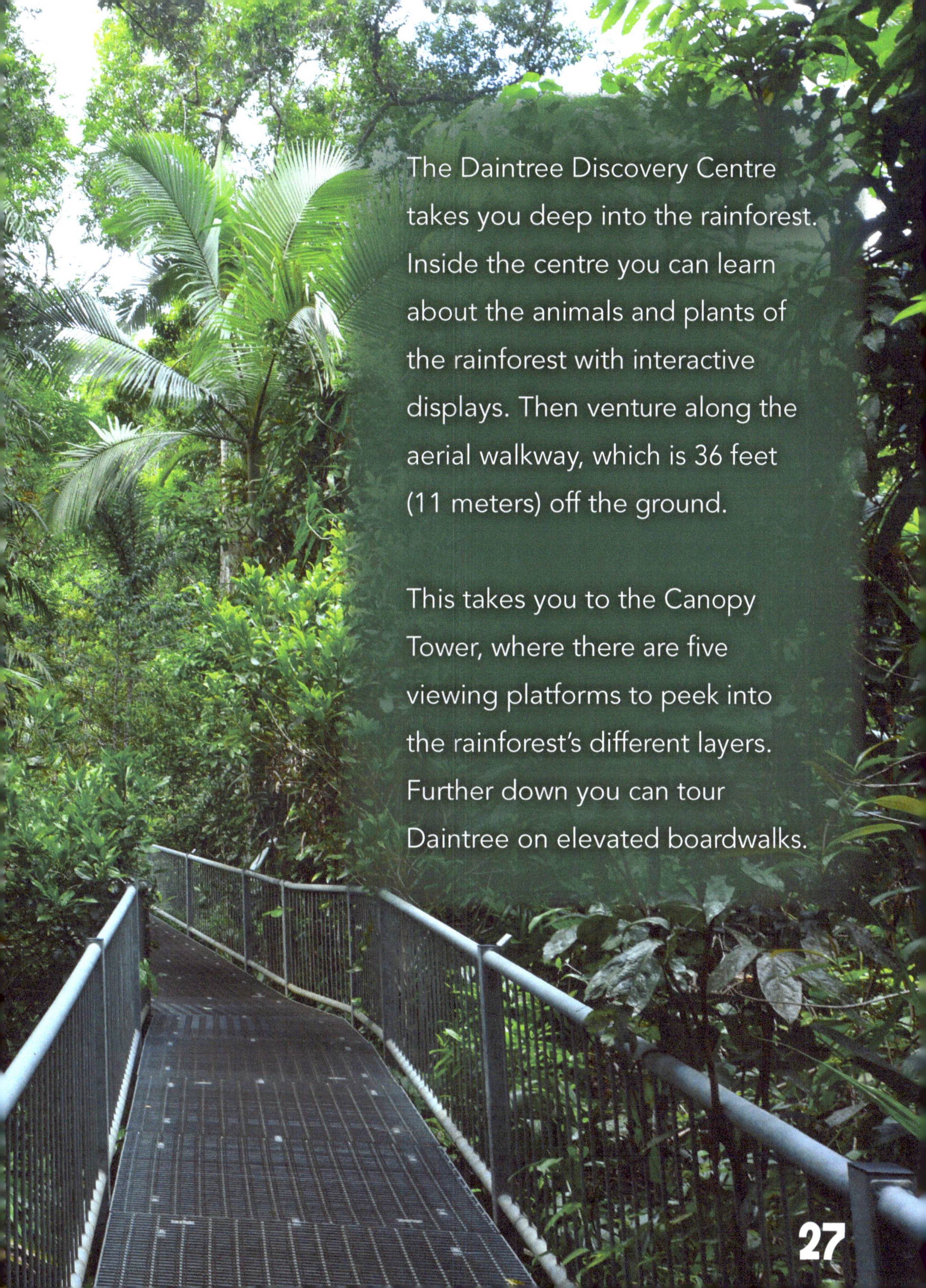

The Daintree Discovery Centre takes you deep into the rainforest. Inside the centre you can learn about the animals and plants of the rainforest with interactive displays. Then venture along the aerial walkway, which is 36 feet (11 meters) off the ground.

This takes you to the Canopy Tower, where there are five viewing platforms to peek into the rainforest's different layers. Further down you can tour Daintree on elevated boardwalks.

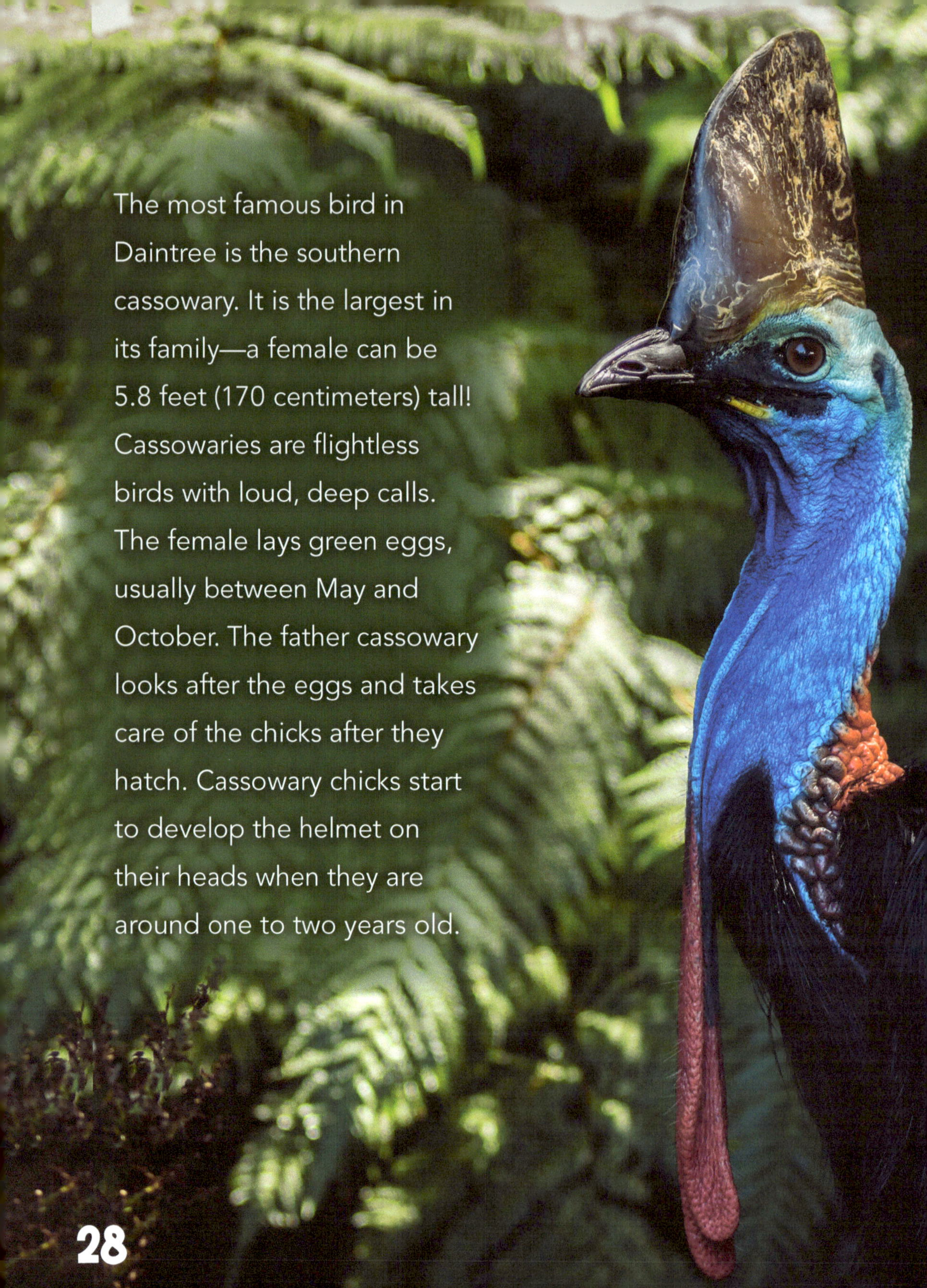

The most famous bird in Daintree is the southern cassowary. It is the largest in its family—a female can be 5.8 feet (170 centimeters) tall! Cassowaries are flightless birds with loud, deep calls. The female lays green eggs, usually between May and October. The father cassowary looks after the eggs and takes care of the chicks after they hatch. Cassowary chicks start to develop the helmet on their heads when they are around one to two years old.

Southern cassowaries are endangered,
and Daintree helps to protect them.
The birds can be difficult to see because
their feathers are very dark. But cassowaries
are active during the day, so you might
spot one looking for food. Never feed
the cassowary or any other animals while
visiting the rainforest.

You will have to look closely to find some of Daintree's other special animals. The musky rat-kangaroo is the smallest of all kangaroos. These little animals have lived in Australia for more than 20 million years. You might see a musky rat-kangaroo early in the morning or evening as it bounds across the forest floor. You are less likely to see a ring-tailed possum because it is active at night. As you explore Daintree, watch out for saltwater crocodiles and pythons, and do not get close!

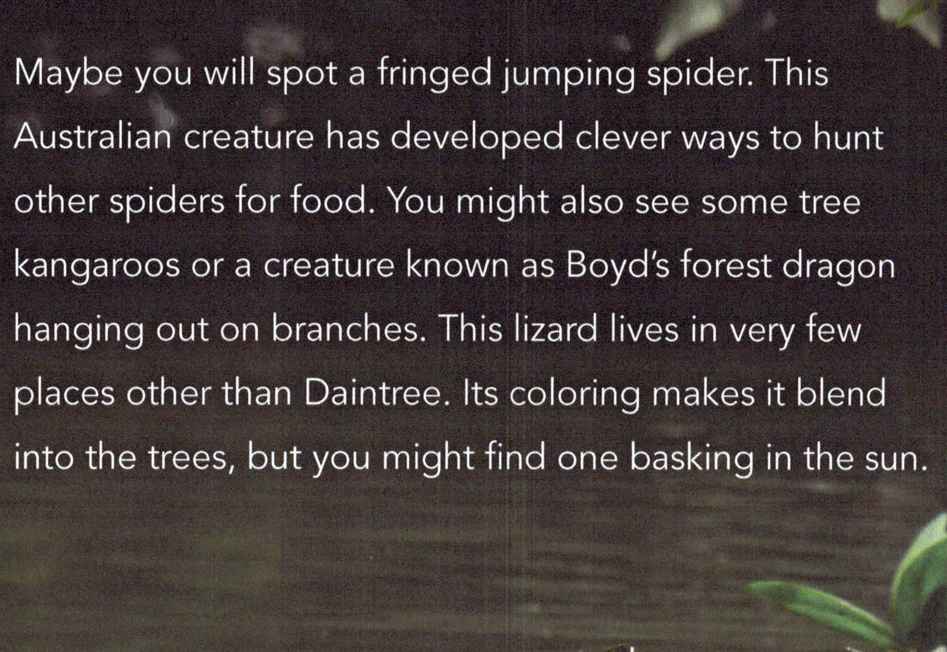

Maybe you will spot a fringed jumping spider. This
Australian creature has developed clever ways to hunt
other spiders for food. You might also see some tree
kangaroos or a creature known as Boyd's forest dragon
hanging out on branches. This lizard lives in very few
places other than Daintree. Its coloring makes it blend
into the trees, but you might find one basking in the sun.

CORCOVADO NATIONAL PARK, COSTA RICA

Corcovado National Park is in southwestern Costa Rica, Central America, near Drake Bay. The park includes tropical rainforest, palm forest, swamps, and beaches. It covers about a third of Costa Rica's Osa Peninsula. Corcovado was created in 1975 to protect the area from logging and mining. You can visit for a day, or you can camp in the park with a permit. Consider visiting between December and April, which are the driest months of the year. October is the rainiest month and the park may be closed.

Exploring Corcovado means a lot of hiking because there are no roads. A guide will accompany you and give you lots of information along the way. There are ranger stations in the park, and you can take many trails from them. You may have to hike to the stations or take a boat.

Corcovado is world famous for its *diverse* (many different kinds) wildlife. It is home to wildcats, such as pumas and jaguars, as well as monkeys, tent-making bats, and many more animals. There are at least 350 different kinds of birds and thousands of species of insects. The park also has hundreds of different kinds of trees, including wild nutmeg and tall silk-cotton trees.

When you visit Corcovado, you will find a rainforest teeming with life. Look for an anteater called a tamandua *(tuh MAN doo wah)* or the coati, a small, insect-eating animal related to the raccoon. See if you can spot the powerful harpy eagle soaring above or perching on a branch in search of lunch.

Peer into the trees to spot a sloth. Sloths are not colorful, but they move very slowly, so you might see one or two hanging in the branches. From afar, watch for American crocodiles and spectacled caimans swimming in the park's rivers or sunning by the shore.

34

Corcovado is famous for several rare species. A guide may help you to find some of them. Even so, you might not see the park's smallest cat, the oncilla, also called the "little tiger cat." Oncillas like to hunt at night. You may hear some animals before you see them. Central American squirrel monkeys are very noisy and live in large groups in the rainforest canopy.

If you are very lucky, you will see a Baird's tapir. This species of tapir is the largest animal in Central America. Baird's tapirs are endangered creatures. Another rare sight is the beautiful resplendent quetzal. This bird was sacred to the ancient Maya and Aztec people who lived in what is today Central America.

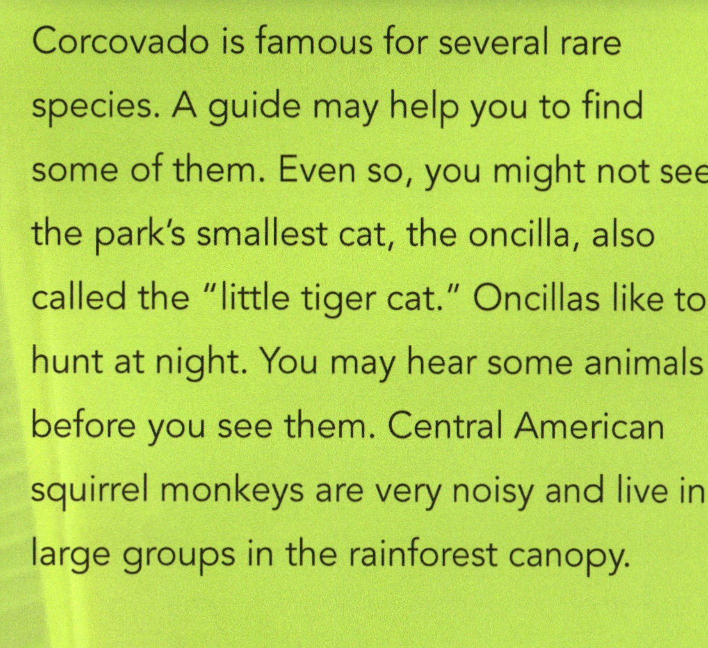

GUNUNG LEUSER NATIONAL PARK, SUMATRA

Some of the most endangered animals in the world live in Gunung Leuser National Park, including the Sumatran orangutan. The mountainous park covers about 3,060 square miles (7,927 square kilometers) in northern Sumatra, Indonesia. Together, Gunung Leuser, Bukit Barisan Selatan, and Kerinci Seblat parks form a UNESCO World Heritage site—the Tropical Rainforest Heritage of Sumatra. The driest time to visit Gunung Leuser is between July and September. There are guided tours that take you to different parts of the park.

More than 130 types of mammals, over 190 different species of reptiles and amphibians, and 380 kinds of birds live in Gunung Leuser. The rainforest is also full of amazing plants. One of the most spectacular is the giant Rafflesia, the biggest flower in the world. It can grow to three feet (0.9 meters) across and weigh up to 15 pounds (6.8 kilograms).

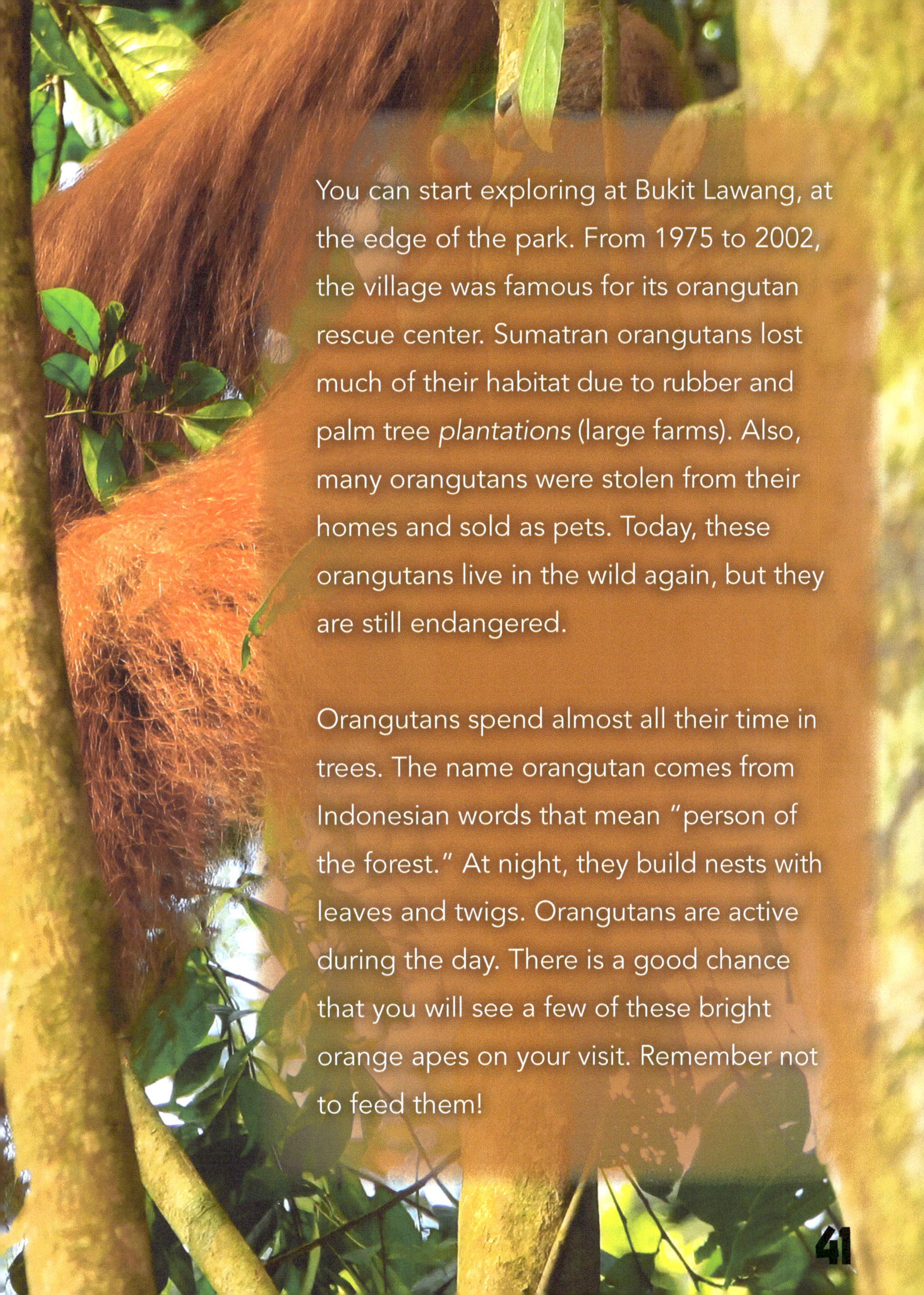

You can start exploring at Bukit Lawang, at the edge of the park. From 1975 to 2002, the village was famous for its orangutan rescue center. Sumatran orangutans lost much of their habitat due to rubber and palm tree *plantations* (large farms). Also, many orangutans were stolen from their homes and sold as pets. Today, these orangutans live in the wild again, but they are still endangered.

Orangutans spend almost all their time in trees. The name orangutan comes from Indonesian words that mean "person of the forest." At night, they build nests with leaves and twigs. Orangutans are active during the day. There is a good chance that you will see a few of these bright orange apes on your visit. Remember not to feed them!

Endangered Sumatran elephants are native to the island. Sumatran elephants are a type of Asian elephant that used to live over a much larger area than they do currently. Like the orangutans, the elephants lost much of their habitat. *Poaching* (illegal hunting or capturing) has also been a problem. You can visit the protected elephants at the Tangkahan Elephant Sanctuary in Gunung Leuser National Park.

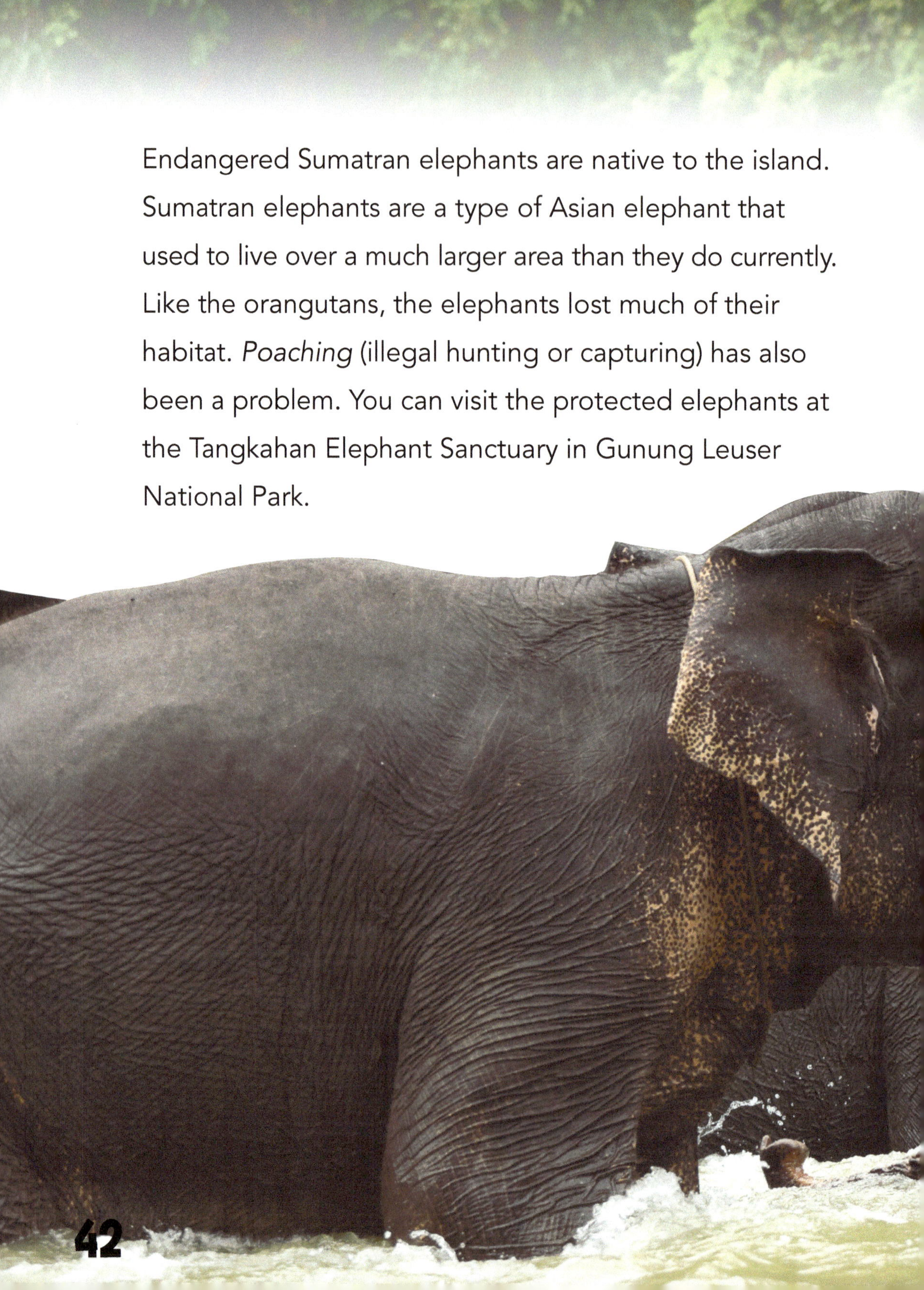

When you hike through the park, you might see a leatherback turtle, such birds as the hornbill, or a bright red dragonfly. Search the trees to see if you can spot a Thomas's leaf monkey. It might be more difficult to see some of the park's other endangered animals. The park helps protect black gibbons, Sumatran tigers, and Sumatran rhinos.

OTHER RAINFORESTS TO VISIT

You can visit many other rainforests around the world. Here are some of them:

Tongass National Forest, Southeast Alaska, United States

A lush old forest where you will find wild salmon, deer, and wolves.

Great Bear Rainforest, British Columbia, Canada

Here you might spot the rare spirit bear. Sea otters and grizzlies also live here.

Monteverde Cloud Forest, Costa Rica

Low clouds create a misty environment where orchids and many other plants grow. Such animals as salamanders and armadillos live here.

Manu National Park, Peru

About 850 different species of birds live in this rainforest, as well as pumas and giant otters.

Yanoda Rainforest, near Sanya, Hainan province, China

There is an amazing glass viewing platform over the forest, or you can hike to see waterfalls, plants, and animals.

Khai Yai National Park, Thailand

You will probably see an elephant or two when you visit this park. There are also reptiles, such as the Chinese water dragon, and birds, like the hornbill.

Nyungwe National Park, Rwanda, Africa

Chimpanzees, mongoose, butterflies, and monkeys live in this African rainforest.

READING FOCUS

Text Structure is all about the way a text is organized. When we know the structure, we can focus more of our energy and attention on comprehending what we read.

This book uses a Description Text Structure. It describes a topic and its characteristics using details, adjectives, and a logical order. Description texts often use examples to show and explain the main idea or topic.

Description texts usually include a lot of interesting details. We can use a graphic organizer to help us keep track of the most important information.

1. This is a Bubble Diagram, a strong graphic organizer for Description texts. Visit **www.worldbook.com/ resources** to download and print copies or create your own!

2. As you read and/or revisit the text, complete a Bubble Diagram for EACH section:
   - What Is a Rain Forest?
   - Tambopata National Reserve, Peru
   - Daintree National Park, Australia
   - Corcovado National Park, Costa Rica
   - Gunung Leuser National Park, Sumatra

3. For each section, write the title in the center-most bubble. Next, add important details to the bubbles attached to that central, main idea. Remember, you do not have enough bubbles for *every* detail. Think critically to determine which details to include.

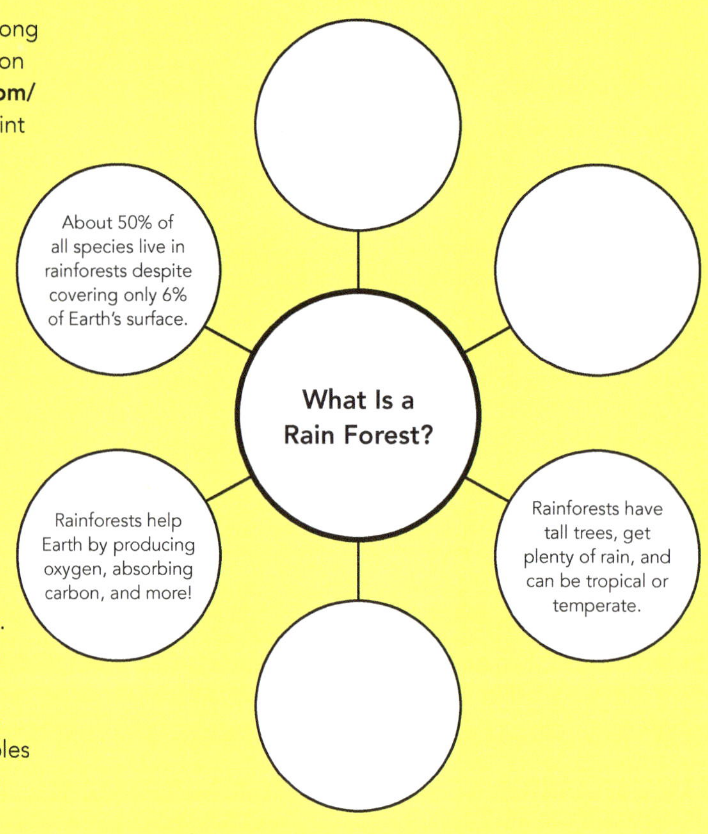

What other information about visiting a rain forest will you add to your Bubble Diagram?

WRITING FOCUS

What do YOU think?

In your opinion, which of the four spotlighted locations would be best for visiting a rain forest?

Review the notes you took on your Bubble Diagrams. Use evidence from the text, supported by logical reasoning, to answer the question. Your writing should include:

- A **hook** where you grab your readers' attention
- A **thesis statement** where you state your opinion
- At least 3 **reasons** why that is your opinion
- At least 3 **details** that support each reason

Use an Opinion Writing Graphic Organizer to sort through your thoughts before you write your response. Create your own or download and print a version from **www.worldbook.com/resources.**

Opinion Writing Graphic Organizer

Hook and Thesis:

Reason #1	Detail #1
	Detail #2
	Detail #3
Reason #2	Detail #1
	Detail #2
	Detail #3
Reason #3	Detail #1
	Detail #2
	Detail #3

You might have noticed some words in this book written in *italics*. That means they are vocabulary terms! **Challenge yourself!** Can you include at least 5 of these words in your opinion writing?

INDEX

ACKNOWLEDGMENTS

Cover: © Teo Tarras, Shutterstock
TP: © Teo Tarras, Shutterstock
6–7 © Teo Tarras, Shutterstock
8–9 © leandromery, Shutterstock
10–11 © Ondrej Prosicky, Shutterstock; © dangdumrong, Shutterstock
12–13 © Gudkov Andrey, Shutterstock; © Sergey Uryadnikov, Shutterstock
14–15 © Luca Lanfranchi, Shutterstock
16–17 © Louis-Michel Desert, Shutterstock
18–19 © Blue Planet Archive AAF, Alamy
20–21 © Salparadis, Shutterstock
22–23 © Adalbert Dragon, Shutterstock; © Kletr, Shutterstock
24–25 © Jan Korba, Shutterstock
26–27 © ChameleonsEye, Shutterstock
28–29 © Torsten Pursche, Shutterstock
30–31 © Enot Poluskuns, Shutterstock
32–33 © Vaclav Sebek, Shutterstock
34–35 © Zach Holmes, Alamy
36–37 © Miguel Schmitter, Shutterstock; © Salparadis, Shutterstock
38–39 © Marco L, Shutterstock; © Mazur Travel, Shutterstock
40–41 © Don Mammoser, Shutterstock
42–43 © Choups, Alamy
44–45 © Jennifer Kurt Photography, Shutterstock